NATIONAL PARKS A TO Z

ADVENTURE *from* ACADIA *to* ZION!

BY GUS D'ANGELO

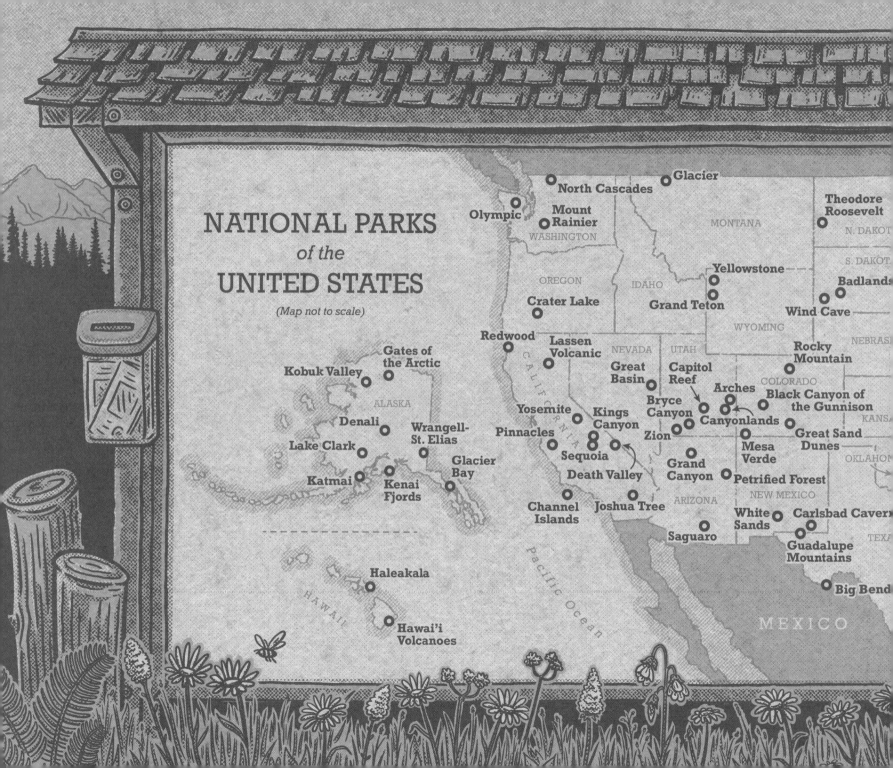

NATIONAL PARKS
of the
UNITED STATES
(Map not to scale)

North Cascades

Glacier

Olympic

Mount Rainier

WASHINGTON

MONTANA

Theodore Roosevelt

N. DAKOT

OREGON

IDAHO

S. DAKOT

Crater Lake

Yellowstone

Badlands

Grand Teton

Wind Cave

WYOMING

NEBRAS

Redwood

Lassen Volcanic

NEVADA

UTAH

Rocky Mountain

Gates of the Arctic

Kobuk Valley

Great Basin

Capitol Reef

COLORADO

ALASKA

Arches

Black Canyon of the Gunnison

KANS.

Yosemite

Kings Canyon

Bryce Canyon

Canyonlands

Denali

Wrangell-St. Elias

Pinnacles

Zion

Great Sand Dunes

OKLAHOM

Lake Clark

Sequoia

Mesa Verde

Katmai

Kenai Fjords

Glacier Bay

Death Valley

Grand Canyon

Petrified Forest

NEW MEXICO

ARIZONA

Channel Islands

Joshua Tree

White Sands

Carlsbad Cavern

Saguaro

TEXA

Haleakala

Guadalupe Mountains

Pacific Ocean

HAWAII

Big Bend

Hawai'i Volcanoes

MEXICO

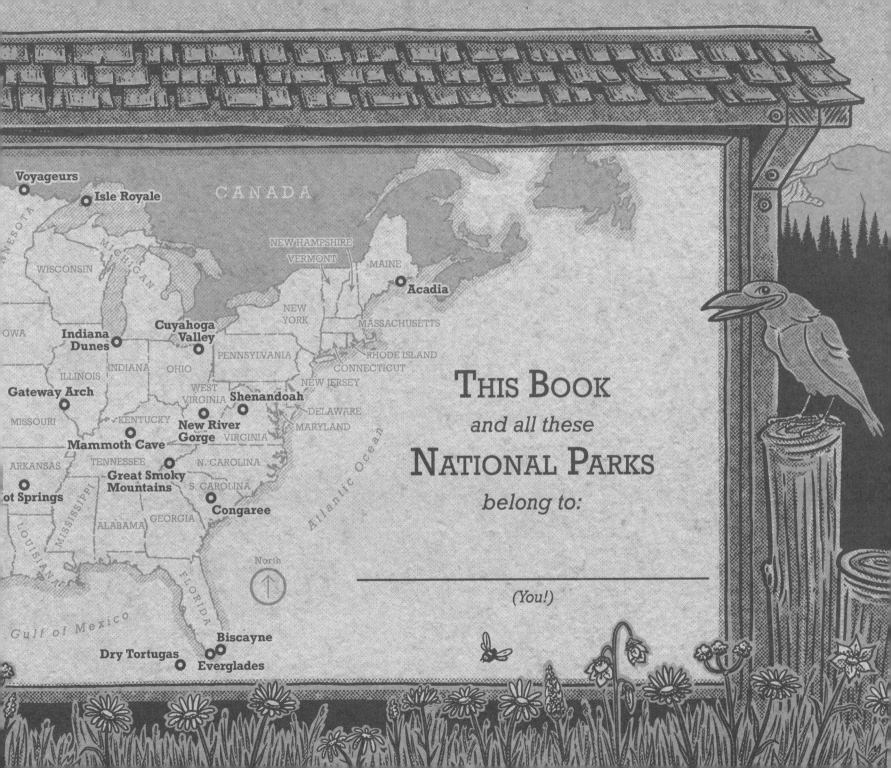

THIS BOOK
and all these
NATIONAL PARKS
belong to:

_____

(You!)

A

An avocet awakes in Acadia.

Acadia National Park is on Maine's rocky Atlantic coast. In wintertime, Cadillac Mountain—which at 1,530 feet is the highest point on the Eastern Seaboard—is where the sun first rises upon the United States. Meanwhile, down on the shoreline, avocets use their extra-long, upturned bills to dig bugs out of the ocean surf.

A is for arrowhead, the National Park Service (NPS) logo. Since 1916, the NPS has protected and preserved the magnificent public parks we all share.

The arrowhead shape represents the history of the land, the bison symbolizes the wildlife, the tree stands for the forests and plants, and the mountain and water reflect the scenery and recreation.

Most of all, the NPS logo represents *you*, because these parks belong to all of us. We need to work together to protect and preserve these special places today so they'll be here for us to enjoy tomorrow.

A bison backpacks into the Badlands.

South Dakota's Badlands National Park is so named because its sharp and mazelike ridges, shadeless grasslands, and extreme temperatures are so unforgiving that the Lakota people called the area *mako sica*, or "bad lands." Bring sturdy boots, a hat, sunscreen, and lots of water. And look out for America's largest land animal, the American bison, also called the buffalo, which can be as tall as a refrigerator, can weigh as much as a small car, and, like people, isn't always in a good mood! If you see any, give them plenty of space.

C

A coyote contemplates the cosmos at the Grand Canyon.

The sheer size of Grand Canyon National Park, in Arizona, boggles the mind: the gorge is a mile deep, averages 10 miles across from rim to rim, and is longer than the drive from New York City to Washington, DC! For six million years, the Colorado River has steadily carved out the canyon, exposing its colorful layered bands of rock.

C is for cultural heritage, the human history of the parks—from old structures and religious sites to stories, songs, and traditions. Ancient rock carvings and cliff dwellings offer a peek into what life was like long ago. Special mountains, caves, and river canyons—locations sacred to Indigenous people for millennia—continue

Related to wolves and dogs, the coyote is a clever animal who can adapt to different landscapes. An important character in Indigenous mythology, the coyote is often a trouble-making or comical trickster who can travel between the human and spirit worlds.

to be visited for pilgrimages, ceremonies, and offerings. Hardy pioneers also left traces—weather-beaten homesteads, abandoned mines, and rustic chapels. This living history reminds us of where we came from and how we became who we are today.

A desert rat
descends . . .
descends . . .

The hottest, driest, and lowest of the parks, Death Valley National Park, in California's Mojave Desert, can get as scorching as 130 degrees. And if you could ride an escalator from sea level down to the bottom of the park's Badwater Basin, the lowest point in the United States, you'd be descending for nearly two minutes!

D

**and descends . . .
into Death Valley.**

Desert kangaroo rats can survive in the extreme heat because they can go their entire lives without drinking any water, getting all the moisture they need from the plants they eat.

D is for dark skies, where there are no city lights and you can see infinite stars overhead. Do you see the Milky Way, the faint band of billions of stars arced across the night sky? Or the North Star, which guides travelers through the night? Or maybe nearby planets (they don't twinkle like stars do)—like Venus, bright on the horizon, or rust-colored Mars? *Look! A shooting star! Quick, make a wish!*

An egret eases into the Everglades.

Everglades National Park, which has been called a "river of grass," is made up of vast wetlands created by water slowly flowing across the state of Florida into the Gulf of Mexico. It's the only place on the planet where saltwater crocodiles (V-shaped snouts) and freshwater alligators (U-shaped snouts) live side by side. It's also a top spot to see birds like great egrets, which stand motionless in shallow water, waiting . . . waiting . . . and waiting . . . until suddenly, with their long yellow bills, they snap up fish to eat!

A tufted puffin frames a photo at Kenai Fjords.

At Alaska's Kenai Fjords National Park, massive rivers of ice meet the sea, slowly grinding, inch by inch, through rock to create numerous fjords—deep glacier-carved canyons now filled with seawater. When diving underwater for small fish to eat, tufted puffins propel themselves by beating their wings and steering with their feet.

F is for fossils, preserved remains of ancient life, like bones, shells, or footprints. Did you find a fossil lying on the ground or imprinted in a rock? Maybe it's from a dinosaur or a saber-toothed cat! Don't touch it; take a photo, and tell a ranger what you found.

A grizzly gasps on Going-to-the-Sun Road at Glacier.

Glacier National Park's cliff-hugging Going-to-the-Sun Road winds up, up, up, up to Logan Pass (6,646 feet) and over the mountainous Continental Divide. Rivers west of the divide flow toward the Pacific Ocean, and rivers east of it flow toward the Atlantic. The park is named after its many glaciers—huge masses of ice created when snow accumulates faster than it can melt. When you're hiking along Glacier's trails, clap, sing, or yell out occasionally so you don't surprise a grizzly bear—it's for your safety and the bear's!

G is for Gracie the border collie, Glacier's "Bark Ranger"! She shoos mountain goats and bighorn sheep out of parking lots, reminding both the animals and people to keep a safe distance apart. Gracie says to stay at least 25 yards away from sheep and goats and 100 yards away from bears!

A honu hulas at Hawai'i Volcanoes.

On the edge of Halema'uma'u crater, in Hawai'i Volcanoes National Park, Hawaiians perform a traditional hula dance to honor Pele, the volcano goddess. Because *honu* (Hawaiian for "green sea turtles") travel on both land and water, they are a historical symbol for the Hawaiian people's connection with the islands and the Pacific Ocean.

H is for homelands. Since long before America's creation, Tribal Nations have lived on these lands, hundreds of highly organized societies with traders, farmers, builders, and craftspeople, from the Calusa of the Everglades to the Ahwahnechee of Yosemite.

An indigo bunting inches across the ice to Isle Royale.

The remote islands of Michigan's Isle Royale National Park are surrounded by the cold, stormy waters of Lake Superior. Winters get so freezing that ice bridges can form on the lake and wolves will walk across from Minnesota! Indigo buntings, who migrate to Isle Royale from Mexico in springtime, aren't actually blue; their feathers are black. It's how our eyes perceive the light reflected by their feathers that makes the birds appear vibrant blue.

A jackrabbit jams at Joshua Tree.

Where the Mojave and Colorado Deserts meet in Southern California is Joshua Tree National Park and its Joshua trees. With their fantastical twisty branches and spiky leaves, they look like something drawn by Dr. Seuss! Equally funky rock formations attract climbers, who "jam" by inserting and twisting a hand or foot into a rock crack to create a secure hold. The black-tailed jackrabbit's enormous ears aren't just for hearing—they also radiate heat, helping to keep the jackrabbit cool in the baking desert temperatures.

A killer whale kayaks at Katmai.

Katmai National Park is a remote Alaskan wilderness of glacier-covered volcanoes and ash-filled valleys. Standing at the top of Brooks Falls, brown bears try to snag jumping salmon with their mouths. Also fond of salmon are killer whales, or orcas, who are not technically whales; with teeth, beaked mouths, and the ability to use sonar to locate nearby objects, they're the largest species of the dolphin family.

A mountain lion lassos lava bombs at Lassen.

At Lassen Volcanic National Park in California, you can hike up volcanoes and see charred lava "bombs" from past eruptions. And you can (cautiously!) explore alien geothermal landscapes of boiling mud pots and steaming vents of sulfur that smell like rotten eggs. Unlike other large cats, mountain lions, also known as cougars or pumas, don't roar—they growl, hiss, and even purr like house cats!

L is for legacy, like that of young Materson Bransford, who in 1838 began guiding tours of Mammoth Cave—he was only a teenager and was enslaved.

1867

1838

1893

1908

2020

From exploring new passages to fighting for freedom and helping inspire a new national park, five generations of Mat's proud descendants have led visitors out of the dark.

M

A mole maneuvers from mystery into . . .

... majesty at Mammoth Cave!

M is for
mystery
and exploring
the unknown:

What's over
that ridge?
Is that a
dinosaur bone?

What's down
that trail?
What's this
footprint I found?

How deep is
that cave?
Uhhh ...
Wh-wh-what was
that sound?

Created over millions of years by water slowly wearing away limestone, Kentucky's Mammoth Cave National Park is a 3D swiss-cheese maze with over 400 miles of passages, tubes, and shafts. It's the largest known cave network in the world. The short, soft hair of eastern moles can lie forward or backward, making it easier for them to slip back and forth through their underground tunnels.

A newt navigates by the night sky in North Cascades.

The Picket Range in Washington's North Cascades National Park is so steep and jagged the names of the peaks sound like they're from a horror film: Mount Fury! Mount Terror! Phantom Peak! Poltergeist Pinnacle! And the star of this film would have to be the tiny eight-inch-long rough-skinned newt, whose skin contains a toxic nerve poison. Don't touch one! But if you do, don't touch your eyes, nose, or mouth!

An owl oohs and aahs at Olympic.

There's so much rain at Olympic National Park, on Washington's Pacific Coast, that lush green ferns and mosses blanket the Hoh Rain Forest, creating an enchanting, emerald wonderland. Above the damp soil, towering Sitka spruce trees interlock their roots like friends supporting each other. Northern spotted owls hunt at night, swallowing their prey whole and then regurgitating small pellets of bone, hair, and skin they can't digest.

A *Peponapis* bee packs it out at Pinnacles.

Pinnacles National Park is named after the rock spires, or pinnacles, that rise up sharply from the mountains of California's Central Valley. The *Peponapis* bee, or squash bee, is one of hundreds of different kinds of bees buzzing around the park, making it home to the widest diversity of bees in the United States.

P is for "Pack it in, pack it out!" Keep our parks clean by carrying out everything you carry in. Don't leave any bottles or bags. Or wrappers, tissues, or orange peels (or even toilet paper or poop—ick!).

When hiking or camping, can you leave it so no one can tell you were there?

A quail quests for quiet at Sequoia.

California's Sequoia and Kings Canyon National Parks are home to the giant sequoias, the largest trees in the world. A single tree can grow as high as a 26-story apartment building and so wide it would take more than 15 people holding hands to reach all the way around it. Being in a grove of these towering giants can feel as peaceful as being inside an old cathedral, mosque, or synagogue. Drooping over the California quail's head is a unique plume that looks like one big feather, but it's actually six feathers clumped together.

R

A ram, raccoon, and red-tailed hawk recite the Junior Ranger pledge at Rocky Mountain.

As you hike up the sky-high, snowcapped mountains in Colorado's Rocky Mountain National Park, the temperature gets cooler and you'll see different animals and plants. Down low you'll see red-tailed hawks, raccoons, and sweet-smelling ponderosa pines, while up high you might spot bighorn sheep in the treeless alpine tundra.

R is for rangers! National park rangers are the friendly guardians of these treasured lands we share.

Interpretive rangers can help you decide which trail to take, show you how to ID a fossil, or point out wildlife.

Nearly every national park has a Junior Ranger program, with an activity booklet of fun quizzes, puzzles, and challenges specific to that park. Once you complete the booklet, share your answers with a park ranger. Then take the Junior Ranger pledge and get a badge! Each park has its own badge—how many can you collect?

 Law-enforcement rangers keep our parks safe and sound, keeping an eye on everything from backcountry trails to busy campgrounds.

Rangers are everyday heroes who protect and preserve. Maybe someday you, too, will wear the flat hat!

A salamander struts over a stream at Great Smoky Mountains.

Great Smoky Mountains National Park, straddling Tennessee and North Carolina, is the most visited national park in the country. Its mist-covered hills and dense hollows were home to mountain people whose old-time fiddle music inspired bluegrass and country. The park is also the salamander capital of the world, home to 30 different species, like the lungless red-cheeked salamander, which breathes through its skin!

S is for staff! Alongside park rangers, many other skilled and passionate people work in our parks: trail crews, firefighters, administrators, and archeologists.

T

A trout treks to the top of Grand Teton.

Sharp as shark fins, the peaks of Grand Teton National Park, in Wyoming, attract mountaineers from around the world. To summit the tallest one, Grand Teton—which at nearly 14,000 feet tall is the height at which skydivers commonly jump out of planes—you'll need the proper gear (a helmet, rope, and an ice axe), along with some courage and climbing lessons! Swimming down below in the Snake River is the native cutthroat trout, so named for the red slash under its lower jaw.

Maintenance workers, preservationists, engineers, and biologists.

Every day, they're out there, caring for our parks. When you see them at work, stop and say, "Thanks!"

An unprepared iguana unravels at Saguaro.

Saguaro National Park, in Arizona's Sonoran Desert, is home to the giant saguaro cactus, which can grow as high as a telephone pole and whose pleated sides can expand like an accordion to absorb more water when it rains. The desert iguana's scientific name is *Dipsosaurus*, from the Greek words *dipsa* and *sauros*, meaning "thirsty lizard." So how much water should you drink so *you* don't unravel when hiking in the dry desert? At least one quart per hour of hiking.

A vulture ventures across Voyageurs.

Voyageurs National Park is a string of lakes and islands along Minnesota's Canadian border. Voyageurs were French-Canadian traders who in the eighteenth century sang songs as they paddled from lake to lake in birchbark canoes built by the Indigenous Ojibwe people. Turkey vultures soar in circles, their black-and-white two-tone wings locked in a V angle, as they scan the ground below for something dead to eat.

A weasel wanders into Wind Cave.

South Dakota's Wind Cave National Park is made up of two worlds: Above ground you'll see wide-open prairies dotted with buffalo and pronghorn. And in Wind Cave below ground, you'll find spectacular natural decorations that look like popcorn and delicate, pointy needles created by slowly seeping water. At the cave's opening, the difference in air pressure creates gusts that will blow your hat off! The black-footed ferret, a weasel with a dark "bandit mask" over its eyes, hunts prairie dogs at night—and sleeps in their abandoned burrows during the day.

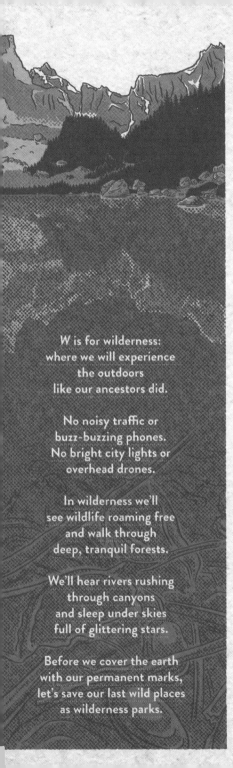

W is for wilderness:
where we will experience
the outdoors
like our ancestors did.

No noisy traffic or
buzz-buzzing phones.
No bright city lights or
overhead drones.

In wilderness we'll
see wildlife roaming free
and walk through
deep, tranquil forests.

We'll hear rivers rushing
through canyons
and sleep under skies
full of glittering stars.

Before we cover the earth
with our permanent marks,
let's save our last wild places
as wilderness parks.

A xerophilous pyrrhuloxia explores Big Bend in Texas.

Big Bend National Park is on West Texas's border with Mexico, so when you paddle down the Rio Grande, the river that winds through the park's narrow, looming canyons, the United States is on your left, and Mexico is on your right. The pint-sized pyrrhuloxia, or desert cardinal, is a xerophilous (from the Greek words *xeros* and *philos*, meaning "dry loving") songbird who sings with a cheerful *chirp-chirp-chirp.*

A yellow-bellied marmot yells at Yellowstone . . . .

. . . while a Yuma myotis yawns at Yosemite!

California's Yosemite National Park is home to the famous El Capitan and Half Dome rock formations, as well as numerous waterfalls, like thundering Yosemite Falls and wispy Bridalveil Fall. It can take several days for climbers to summit "El Cap," so they have to sleep in portaledge tents, which hang off the steep rock face. In early evening, small Yuma myotis bats can fully stuff themselves on beetles, termites, and moths in only 15 minutes!

In 1872, Yellowstone National Park—located where Wyoming, Idaho, and Montana meet—became the world's first national park. It's home to hundreds of gushing geysers—underground hot springs of boiling water that can shoot out spray as high as the Statue of Liberty! While hibernating from September to April, the yellow-bellied marmot lowers its body temperature to just a few degrees above freezing and breathes only two times per minute.

Y is for you, our national parks superhero! In the parks, you fight for what's right by carrying out what you carry in, hiking only on trails, watching wildlife from a distance, and leaving flowers and fossils untouched. At home, you defend our parks from afar by recycling and reusing, turning off faucets and lights, and combating climate change by walking or riding your bike. Teamed up with your fellow superheroes, NPS rangers and staff, you proudly protect our precious public lands. From Acadia to Zion, our champion is you!

A zebra-tailed lizard zonks out at Zion.

At Utah's Zion National Park, you can hike through the Narrows, a 16-mile-long gorge with rock walls so high and close they nearly block out the sky. Before venturing inside, however, check the weather forecast for any recent rains or flash flood warnings. Zebra-tailed lizards are speedy four-inch-long desert dwellers that tolerate heat so well they can chill out in the midday sun, while other lizards need to run for the shade!

Learn More About Our National Parks

National Park Foundation

Established in 1967 by an act of Congress, the National Park Foundation is the official charitable partner of the National Park Service, raising private funds to support NPS activities and services. Much of their work and grants are directed toward engaging and educating youth of all backgrounds, providing them with the opportunity to experience first-hand the wonder of our parks, and inspiring the next generation of park stewards. **nationalparks.org**

National Park Service (NPS)

The NPS is our nation's federal agency entrusted with protecting our most iconic public lands. The NPS manages over 400 "units," which include not only the national parks (generally designated as such for their natural beauty, variety of resources, and large land or water areas) but also national seashores, memorials, monuments, and other notable sites across the country. Here's where to start before planning to visit any of them: **nps.gov/index.htm.**

NPS Accessibilty

For information on accessibility within the national parks, including an interactive map with links to each park's accessible features and activities: **nps.gov/subjects/accessibility /index.htm.**

NPS App

The official NPS app provides interactive maps, self-guided tours, accessibility info, virtual postcards, and much more. NPS rangers and staff constantly update it with new features to help you enjoy the parks. For the links to download it for free, visit: **nps.gov/subjects/digital/nps-apps.htm.**

NPS Junior Ranger Program

Yes! You too can be a Junior Ranger and join the National Park Service "family" committed to preserving and protecting our national parks. Most parks have Junior Ranger programs with fun learning activities special to each park. Go to the park, do the activities, and get that park's Junior Ranger badge! How many can you collect? Explore! Learn! Protect! **nps.gov/kids/become-a-junior-ranger.htm.**

NPS Kids in Parks

Are you a kid about to visit a national park? For advice from rangers, hiking tips, camping suggestions, online activities, tours, and more, here's where to start planning your next adventure! **nps.gov/kids/index.htm.**

NPS Resources for Educators

With endless opportunities to learn about and directly experience nature, science, history, and much, much more, the parks are "America's largest classroom." Educators can go here for a wealth of information about lesson plans, field experiences, classroom materials, and more: **nps.gov/teachers/index.htm.**

National Geographic Kids: National Parks

The legendary magazine's fun National Parks portal for kids, with videos, quizzes, and more: **kids.nationalgeographic .com/nature/topic/national-parks.**

Nat Geo also has a comprehensive list of books, websites, and videos for kids: **nationalgeographic.org/idea/national -park-resources/.**

Learn More About Leave No Trace (LNT)

Remember that LNT applies to toilet paper and poop too! Bury your poop at least 6 to 8 inches deep and 200 feet from water or, better yet, pack it out in a biodegradable doggie poop bag. And *always* carry out your TP! To learn more: **lnt.org.**

Thanks

To all the rangers, staff, friends, and family who inspired and supported me: AnniAbbi & Hustlin' Hank; Lyle Balenquah; Joel Barshak; Mark Biel and Gracie the Bark Ranger; Paul Connolly; Daisy D; Keli Dailey; Michael Daly; John Dell'Osso; Dale Dualan; Lisa Duff; the Duff family editors; "F-stop" Flynn; Dan Fost; John, Jennifer, Bealena, and Giacomo Giustina; Kevin Gottesman; Tran Ha; Michael Hearst; James and Rico; JSK '14; Jay Kassabian; Melissa Kelleher; Jeff and Tina Kroot; Mike Laycock; Andrew Losowsky; Rita Martin; Scott Martin; Neil "MacGyver" McEleney; Joan M. Meiners; Andrew S. Muñoz; Garvin O'Neil; Hal O'Neil; Shirley Owen; Pablo, Dave, and Diego; Katie Pell; Andy Porter; Martín Quiroga; Andy Rosa; Saxton family; Molly Schroer; Greg Scott; Camille Seaman; Lauren Spier; Tracy and Ed; Turuc family; and Jessica Yaquinto.

To all the adventurers at BORP, with special thanks to Bonnie Lewkowicz for her enthusiasm and guidance.

To Alexis and Kai at Tides for giving me some space.

To everyone at the North Cascades Institute, in particular Evan Holmstrom for my residency and Mari Schramm for my "editing workshops" with the kids of Mountain School.

Special thanks to Ashleigh Thompson whose expertise refined the themes of this book; Jason Nez who led me to the edge of the Grand Canyon—and a new way of perceiving our parks and nation; Matt "Send it!" Tilford, mountain biker, adventurer, and activist; Eduardo Balaguer for keeping the 4x4 running; and to Jerry Bransford, who graciously guided me in the footsteps of his ancestors.

To artists Tracy Cox, John "It's the Details" Blanchard, and Arena Reed.

To Pete D'Angelo, lifelong art co-conspirator, who never thinks my lines are thick enough.

To everyone at Mountaineers Books, in particular: Kate Rogers, Janet Kimball, Janice Lee, and Jen Grable.

To Danielle Svetcov and the team at Levine Greenberg Rostan Literary Agency.

And finally . . . to Jennifer, whose wacky energy entertains and inspires me every day, I lovingly dedicate this book—even though she hates camping.

About the Author

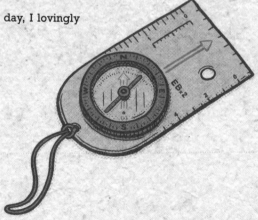

GUS D'ANGELO first fell in love with the outdoors as a child, hiking, fishing, and snowshoeing with his three brothers on his family's farm in Michigan's Upper Peninsula. These early adventures led to his passion for public lands and his hope that all young people get to experience the thrill, mystery, and solitude of the outdoors. Gus is an illustrator and animator who now lives in San Francisco with his partner, filmmaker Jennifer Kroot.

"Screens off! Adventure on!"

MOUNTAINEERS BOOKS is dedicated to the exploration, preservation, and enjoyment of outdoor and wilderness areas.

1001 SW Klickitat Way, Suite 201, Seattle, WA 98134
800-553-4453, www.mountaineersbooks.org

Printed in Canada
Distributed in the United Kingdom by Cordee, www.cordee.co.uk
26 25 24 23   2 3 4 5 6

Copyeditor: Janice Lee
Design and illustrations: Gus D'Angelo
Design and layout: Jen Grable

Library of Congress Cataloging-in-Publication data is on file for this title at https://lccn.loc.gov/2021057770

♻ Printed on 30% recycled paper and FSC-certified materials with vegetable-based inks

FSC
www.fsc.org

MIX
Paper from responsible sources
FSC® C016245

ISBN (hardcover): 978-1-68051-587-9

An independent nonprofit publisher since 1960

MOUNTAINEERS BOOKS, including its two imprints, Skipstone and Braided River, is a leading publisher of quality outdoor recreation, sustainability, and conservation titles. As a 501(c)(3) nonprofit, we are committed to supporting the environmental and educational goals of our organization by providing expert information on human-powered adventure, sustainable practices at home and on the trail, and preservation of wilderness.

Our publications are made possible through the generosity of donors, and through sales of 700 titles on outdoor recreation, sustainable lifestyle, and conservation. To donate, purchase books, or learn more, visit us online at www.mountaineersbooks.org.

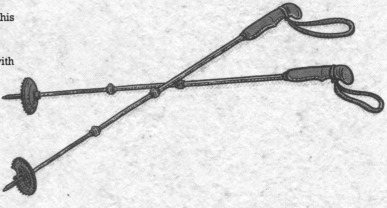